Searchlight
BOOKS™

What
Are Earth's
Cycles?

Investigating

Animal
Life Cycles

L. J. Amstutz

Lerner Publications ◆ Minneapolis

Content Consultant: Mark Davis, Professor of Biology, Macalester College

Lerner Publications Company
A division of Lerner Publishing Group, Inc.
241 First Avenue North
Minneapolis, MN 55401 USA

For reading levels and more information, look up this title at www.lernerbooks.com.

Library of Congress Cataloging-in-Publication Data

Amstutz, Lisa J.
    Investigating animal life cycles / by L.J. Amstutz.
        pages cm. — (Searchlight books™. What are earth's cycles?)
    Includes index.
    Audience: Ages 8 to 11.
    Audience: Grades 4 to 6.
    ISBN 978-1-4677-8057-5 (lb : alk. paper) — ISBN 978-1-4677-8331-6
(pb : alk. paper) — ISBN 978-1-4677-8332-3 (eb pdf)
    1. Animal life cycles—Juvenile literature. I. Title.
QL49.A49 2015
571.8—dc23   2015001950

Manufactured in the United States of America
1 – VP – 7/15/15

Contents

Chapter 1

THE CYCLE OF LIFE

Picture a blue egg, a chirping chick, and a bird singing in a tree. What do all these things have in common?

Eggs are the first stage of a robin's life cycle. What are the other stages?

The egg, the chick, and the adult bird are all stages of a robin's life cycle. A life cycle tells the story of an animal's life. It shows how the animal is born and grows up. When the animal starts to reproduce, a new life cycle begins.

THE ADULT AMERICAN ROBIN IS KNOWN FOR ITS REDDISH-ORANGE BREAST.

The great white shark is a member of the fish group.

All Kinds of Animals

Animals come in many shapes and sizes. They live in water and on land. They live in deserts, in rain forests, and even in the icy tundra.

People who study animals put them into groups. These groups include mammals, reptiles, birds, fish, amphibians, and insects. The life cycles of these animals are not all the same. But they all start in the same place. They begin with an embryo.

See the Cycle

A pond is a great place to find animals at various stages of their life cycles. Take a net and skim it along the bottom of a pond. Be careful not to get too much mud in your net. Dump the net into a bucket or pan filled with some clean water. What do you see? Draw pictures of the things you find. Look them up in a pond field guide to identify them.

Chapter 2

AN ANIMAL IS BORN

An embryo is an animal in its very early stages. It starts as a single cell. An embryo can grow inside an egg. Or it can grow inside its mother.

This pig has embryos growing inside her body. What is another way that embryos can grow?

Small animals develop quickly. Chicken embryos grow for about three weeks before they hatch into baby chicks. Larger animals usually develop more slowly. An elephant embryo grows inside its mother for almost two years.

Mosquito eggs hatch in about two days.

Giving Birth

Most mammal embryos grow inside their mothers' bodies. There, they are safe and warm. Nearly all mammals give birth to live young.

A few reptiles, fish, amphibians, and insects give birth to live young. But most of them lay eggs. All birds lay eggs. Two mammals lay eggs as well: the platypus and the echidna.

An echidna is a small mammal of Australia, Tasmania, and New Guinea. Echidnas are also known as spiny anteaters.

Reptile eggs are soft and leathery. Fish and frog eggs are soft like jelly. They float in the water. Bird eggs have a hard shell to protect them.

A baby iguana breaks out of its leathery egg. This reptile is native to Mexico and Central America.

The Incredible Egg

Tiny holes in the shell of a bird egg let air flow in and out. Inside the shell is a thin membrane that keeps out germs. It also keeps the egg from drying out. Inside the membrane are the egg white, yolk, and embryo. The egg white and yolk are food for the growing chick.

An egg is hard for a baby bird to break. So a chick has an egg tooth on top of its beak. This sharp point helps the chick crack the shell. The egg tooth falls off soon after the chick hatches.

LIFE CYCLE OF A CHICKEN

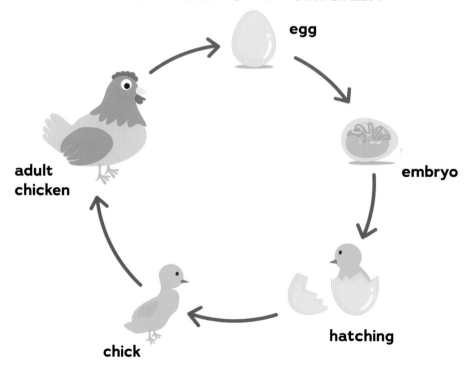

egg

embryo

hatching

chick

adult chicken

See the Cycle

Look closely at a chicken egg. Can you see the tiny airholes in the shell? With an adult's permission, carefully crack the egg into a bowl. Find the egg white and the yolk. Now look at a piece of shell. Find the thin membrane inside. Try peeling it away from the shell. What does it feel like?

THE AMERICAN ALLIGATOR LIVES IN THE SOUTHERN PART OF THE UNITED STATES.

Building a Nest

Some animals build nests for their young. Nests can be made of sticks, mud, plant matter, or fur. A female American alligator builds a huge mound of mud and plants. She hollows out the center of the mud nest and places her eggs inside.

Not all egg layers build nests. The emperor penguin holds its egg on top of its feet. A ladybug places its eggs on a leaf. Most frogs and fish lay masses of eggs in water.

A frog rests on top of its eggs.

Chapter 3

STAGES OF GROWTH

Baby mammals, fish, and birds look much like their parents. They grow bigger but do not change much. Baby reptiles look like their parents too. Most of them molt, or shed their skin, as they grow.

Dogs are mammals, so puppies look similar to their parents. What other animal groups have babies that look similar to their parents?

16

Amphibians and insects change much more as they grow. They change form at each stage of their life cycle. This is called metamorphosis.

Female frogs lay eggs in water. In time, tadpoles hatch from these eggs. A tadpole looks like a little fish. It breathes with gills like a fish. Soon it grows lungs and legs. Its tail disappears. It becomes an adult frog.

This tadpole has grown legs, but it has not yet lost its fish-like tail.

Complete Metamorphosis

Insects such as beetles and butterflies go through a complete metamorphosis. Their life cycle has four stages: egg, larva, pupa, and adult. They change form at each stage.

THESE MEALWORMS ARE THE LARVAL
FORM OF A BEETLE.

LIFE CYCLE OF A BUTTERFLY

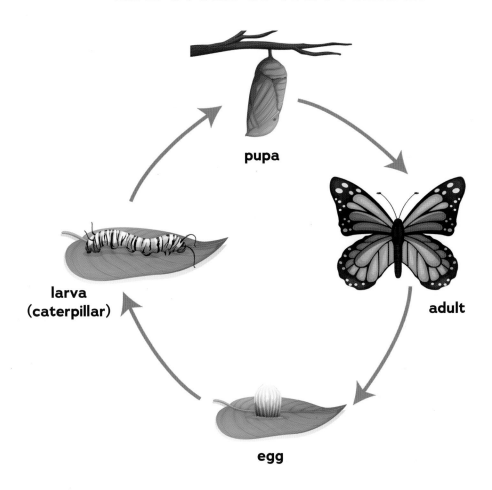

pupa

larva
(caterpillar)

adult

egg

A butterfly starts as an egg. A larva, or caterpillar, hatches from this egg. The caterpillar eats, grows, and molts several times. Then it becomes a pupa. A hard case forms around its body. Inside the case, the insect changes form again. When it leaves the case, it is an adult butterfly. It has wings and is ready to mate.

Termites often live in huge mounds, such as this one in Australia.

Incomplete Metamorphosis

Some insects grow in a different way. Their life cycle has three stages: egg, nymph, and adult. Termites, stinkbugs, and grasshoppers are among this group.

A grasshopper starts out as an egg. In spring, a nymph hatches from the egg. It looks like a tiny adult. But the nymph does not have wings. It molts five or six times as it grows. After its final molt, it is an adult. It can fly and reproduce.

THIS COLORFUL ADULT GRASSHOPPER
HAS GONE THROUGH ITS FINAL MOLT.

Parental Care

Some baby animals are born helpless. Their parents must take care of them. Mammals feed their babies milk. The milk comes from the mother's body.

Birds keep their chicks safe and warm. Some chicks can hunt for food soon after they hatch. Others need their parents to feed them.

A few reptiles, amphibians, and insects care for their young as well. For example, honeybees carefully tend their larvae. They feed them honey, pollen, and a food called royal jelly.

Royal jelly is a white liquid that worker bees produce. It contains protein for the larvae.

See the Cycle

A cow's milk has all the nutrients that its calf needs to grow. To learn what these nutrients are, find a carton of whole milk at the grocery store. Look at the information on the side of the carton. What nutrients are listed? Check the list of ingredients. Have any vitamins been added to the milk?

Baby sea turtles make their way to the water.

On Their Own

Most kinds of insects, reptiles, amphibians, and fish do not feed their young. Their babies must start looking for food right away. Baby sea turtles crawl out of their nests, across the sand, and into the ocean. There, they feed on algae, crabs, fish, and shrimp.

These species tend to lay many eggs so that some will survive. A fish called a sturgeon can lay up to seven million eggs each year. Only a few of these will hatch. Most are eaten by predators, are washed ashore, or are smashed in the tide.

SOME STURGEON CAN GROW UP TO
12 FEET (3.7 METERS) LONG.

▼

Chapter 4

ALL GROWN UP

When an animal is fully grown, it is ready to reproduce. But first, it needs to find a mate. Animals use colors, scents, sounds, and dances to attract mates. The male peacock fans out its colorful tail feathers to impress females. Male goats make a smelly musk that females like. Frogs make loud mating calls.

The bird of paradise does a dance to attract mates. What do some other animals do?

The Mating Process

Once a male and female animal have found each other, they mate. Sperm from the male fertilizes an egg from the female. This egg will become an embryo. It will grow into a new animal.

The sperm and the egg each contain genes. The genes make the animal look and grow a certain way. It will have traits from both its parents.

A baby elephant has genes from both its mother and its father.

Two adult swans swim with their young at the edge of a pond.

After mating, some animals stay together to raise their babies. Others do not. A few, like swans, mate for life. They will raise young together each year until one of the parents dies.

See the Cycle

Look through some of your family's photos. Compare pictures of yourself as a baby, a toddler, and a child. Now look at photos of an adult. Make a list of the differences you see. How do humans change from birth to adulthood?

Other Ways to Reproduce

A few animals can reproduce without a mate. Parts of them may break off and form new animals. For example, sponges can make buds that grow into new sponges. Pieces of starfish can grow into new starfish.

If this starfish loses an arm, a new arm will grow in its place. And the lost arm will grow into a new starfish.

The Komodo dragon is a large lizard that lives in Indonesia. It can develop from an unfertilized egg.

Other animals can develop from unfertilized eggs. Male bees are one example. These new animals have genes only from their mother.

A female chimpanzee may give birth to three or more babies during her lifetime.

Completing the Cycle

Some small animals die soon after mating. But for others, life goes on. They may reproduce many times.

Large animals tend to reproduce slowly. A mother giraffe carries an embryo for fifteen months. Smaller animals breed much faster. A mouse can have up to ten litters per year. There are five or six babies in each litter.

MOTHER ZEBRAS ARE PREGNANT FOR TWELVE TO THIRTEEN MONTHS.

Life Spans

A life span is the length of time an animal can live. A tortoise can live for 150 years. A mayfly lives for only a day or two as an adult.

Some flamingos live for more than forty years.

The dodo bird went extinct in the 1600s.

Not all animals die of old age. Some die of disease or hunger. Others are killed by predators. Still others die when humans destroy their habitat.

Some animals of each species must live long enough to reproduce. Otherwise, they will die out. They will become extinct, like the dinosaurs.

Death and Decay

When an animal dies, its body begins to decay. Insects, fungi, bacteria, and earthworms break it down. Nutrients from the animal's body go back into the soil. They will feed new plants. These, in turn, will feed new animals. In this way, the cycle of life goes on.

An animal's body decays in a field.

Science and the Animal Life Cycle

You can learn a lot about animals by watching them up close. To get a better look, make an insect hotel. First, lay a plastic bottle on its side. Ask an adult to help you cut a 2- by 3-inch (5- by 7.5-centimeter) hole in one flat edge. Put a few leaves, twigs, rocks, and pieces of grass in the bottle. Then lay a piece of screen or netting over the hole. Use duct tape to hold it in place.

Now find an insect you want to watch. Make sure it does not sting or bite! Use the lid of the bottle to gently scoop it inside. Screw the lid on and observe. Write down what you see. What color is your insect? How many legs does it have? Does it have wings? Is it flying around or crawling? Draw a picture of your insect.

Insects cannot live long without food and water. So set your insect free at the end of the day. You can always catch another one tomorrow.

Glossary

decay: to rot or break down

embryo: an animal in its earliest stage of development

extinct: having died out. An animal is extinct when there are no more living members of its kind.

fertilize: to join the male and female cells to form a new embryo

gene: information inside a cell that controls the way a living thing looks and grows

life span: the length of time a plant or an animal lives

litter: a group of young animals born at the same time

metamorphosis: a change in form

molt: to shed feathers or skin and replace them with new ones

predator: an animal that eats other animals

reproduce: to make a new animal

species: a group of animals that are closely related and can breed with one another

sperm: a male reproductive cell

trait: a feature passed on through the genes to offspring

LERNER

SOURCE

Expand learning beyond the printed book. Download free, complementary educational resources for this book from our website, www.lerneresource.com.

Learn More about the Animal Life Cycle

Books

Johnson, Jinny. *Animal Planet Atlas of Animals*. Minneapolis: Millbrook Press, 2012. Amazing facts, helpful maps, and beautiful images make this book an excellent way to learn about animals.

Solway, Andrew. *Secrets of Animal Life Cycles*. New York: Marshall Cavendish Benchmark, 2011. This book answers all your questions about animal life cycles in a question-and-answer format.

Wood, Alix. *Amazing Animal Life Cycles*. New York: Windmill Books, 2013. Lots of amazing facts about animal life cycles give this book its "wow" factor.

Websites

Enchanted Learning: The Life Cycle of a Butterfly
http://www.enchantedlearning.com/subjects/butterfly/lifecycle
This site features printouts and activities that help students understand the life cycle of a butterfly.

Learn the Life Cycle of Animals through Games
http://www.turtlediary.com/kids-games/science/animals/life-cycle-of-animals.html
Learn the life cycle of a frog or a butterfly with Turtle Diary's online games.

National Geographic: **Red-Eyed Tree Frog's Life Cycle**
http://video.nationalgeographic.com/video/frog_greentree_lifecycle
Watch an action-packed video on the life cycle of the red-eyed tree frog.

Index

Photo Acknowledgments

The images in this book are used with the permission of: © D and D Photo Sudbury/Shutterstock Images, p. 4; © Mike Truchon/Shutterstock Images, p. 5; © Alexius Sutandio/Shutterstock Images, p. 6; © Matt Jeppson/Shutterstock Images, p. 7; © pavla/Shutterstock Images, p. 8; © Gallinago media/Shutterstock Images, p. 9; © Hugh Lansdown/Shutterstock Images, p. 10; © bluedogroom/Shutterstock Images, p. 11; © aekikuis/Shutterstock Images, p. 12; © Karen Sarraga/Shutterstock Images, p. 13; © Raffaella Calzoni/Shutterstock Images, p. 14; © Matteo photos/Shutterstock Images, p. 15; © Eric Isselee/Shutterstock Images, p. 16; © Dr. Morley Read/Shutterstock Images, p. 17; © CreativeNature R.Zwerver/Shutterstock Images, p. 18; © BlueRingMedia/Shutterstock Images, p. 19; © Piotr Gatlik/Shutterstock Images, p. 20; © Tyler Fox/Shutterstock Images, p. 21; © Stefano Lunardi/Shutterstock Images, p. 22; © PhotoObjects.net/Thinkstock, p. 23; © FamVeld/Shutterstock Images, p. 24; © Yory Frenklakh/Shutterstock Images, p. 25; © Herianus/iStockphoto, p. 26; © jo Crebbin/Shutterstock Images, p. 27; © Igor Borodin/Shutterstock Images, p. 28; © Blend Images/Shutterstock Images, p. 29; © Vilainecrevette/Shutterstock Images, p. 30; © Sergey Uryadnikov/Shutterstock Images, pp. 31, 32; © Jamen Percy/Shutterstock Images, p. 33; © Seqoya/Shutterstock Images, p. 34; © Photos.com/Thinkstock, p. 35; © IdealPhoto30/iStockphoto, p. 36; © Anest/iStockphoto, p. 37.

Front cover: © iStockphoto.com/GoranKapor.

Main body text set in Adrianna Regular 14/20.
Typeface provided by Chank.